J.S. Bach for Electric Bass

THREE DUETS AND FIVE SOLO PIECES ARRANGED ... AR

by Bob Gallway, PH.D.

CONTENTS

This book is lovingly dedicated
to Karen, my wife; Harry, my dear son;
John Davidson, an advisor, friend, and teacher;
and to J.S.B. for his greatness and inspiration.

ISBN 978-0-634-03143-4

Visit Hal Leonard Online at
www.halleonard.com

INTRODUCTION

Johann Sebastian Bach is one of the greatest musicians of all time. He was born in Germany in 1685, died in 1750, and is classified by historians as a composer of the Baroque period. Musicians from Ludwig van Beethoven to Keith Jarrett have studied Bach, and his works have provided pleasure and inspiration for over two hundred years.

Since their creation, Bach's compositions have been realized on nearly every musical instrument imaginable. Any electric bassist, whether focused on jazz, funk, rock, fusion, etc., is bound to improve technique, as well as musical understanding and appreciation, through mastery of these pieces.

Bach's phenomenal depth of expression and profound sensitivity live in this music. Learn the pieces in this book, and you will be amazed at what a moving experience it is to play them; a shadow of Bach's genius will briefly come alive within you. And hopefully, some of it will linger!

HISTORY

Most of Bach's life was focused on music for the church. However, from 1717 until 1723 he was employed in Cöthen by Prince Leopold as Kappelmeister (church choral conductor) and director of chamber music for the royal court. Prince Leopold loved music and kept a seventeen-piece orchestra at Bach's disposal. During his six years in rural Cöthen, Bach composed an astonishing series of instrumental masterpieces including the Two- and Three-Part Inventions, the six Suites for Solo Cello, Book One of The Well-Tempered Clavier, the French and English Suites for Solo Harpsichord, the six Sonatas for Solo Violin, and the six Brandenburg Concertos. Since Bach was accomplished on various keyboards, violin, and probably cello, it is no surprise that these instrumental compositions tend to feature the instruments he knew best.

THE MUSIC

Except for the Sinfonia from Partita 2, which was written in 1727—and is one of Bach's few compositions published during his lifetime—all the pieces in this book were composed while Bach conducted in Cöthen. The first two duets—Two-Part Inventions 4 and 1—were written in 1723 as studies for performers and composers. The Two-Part Inventions exemplify independent two-part writing, freely using the techniques of fugue and canon without strictly adhering to either. It was Bach's intention to familiarize beginning students of the keyboard with counterpoint as well as right- and left-hand independence. In the Two-Part Inventions, a brief theme is stated and then developed with an awesome array of compositional techniques.

Aside from the Two-Part Inventions, all the pieces in this book are drawn from a popular Baroque musical form called the *suite*, also known as the *sonata* or *partite*. The form originated hundreds of years before the Baroque era, most likely when lutenists arranged popular dances of the day into medleys of tunes in the same or related keys. Because of the varied meter, mood, tempo, and rhythm of each of the dances comprising a suite, Baroque composers found that this form offered great possibility for musical expression, while maintaining the basic formal structure and rhythm of each dance form. For example, the Allemande on page 33 in this book is typical of all such dances, in that it is a slow dance in 4/4 meter with a strikingly ornamental line.

HOW TO USE THIS BOOK

There are many possible approaches to learning the music in this book. If you are an experienced music reader, you probably have a method that works for you. If you are new to this sort of thing, or if your progress seems slow, you may want to try the following suggestions:

1. Figure out a single measure or short phrase and try to play it along with a metronome. Keep slowing down the tempo until you can play the phrase smoothly in time. At this point, don't worry about the proper tempo of the piece; just learn the phrase well enough to play it perfectly with the metronome. Creating a loop out of the phrase often helps, and by playing it repeatedly without a pause between the beginning and the ending, you will learn it quickly. Sometimes a whole phrase or measure is too much to tackle at once. In that case, just try two or three notes or chords until you've mastered them.

2. When you are ready to move on, do the same thing with the next measure or phrase. When you've learned it, try the two sections together. Once you can get through an entire piece, gradually speed up the metronome. If your playing becomes sloppy, you have sped it up too soon. When the entire piece is smooth and up to tempo, the metronome is no longer necessary, and it's time to play it the way you feel it!

Although I have occasionally referred to "proper tempo," Bach never recommended specific metronome settings. By listening to any of the numerous recordings of these compositions on keyboard, violin, or cello, you can find ample suggested tempos (see the discography below).

For each of the duets in this book, music for the second part (accompaniment) is included immediately after the first.

DISCOGRAPHY

The Two-Part Inventions:
1. Gould (piano), Columbia 3S-754.
2. Kirkpatrick (clavichord), Archive 73174 (198 674).
3. Malcolm (harpsichord), Nonesuch 71144.

Partita Number 2 in C Minor for Solo Harpsichord:
1. Fuller (harpsichord), Nonesuch 71176.
2. Gould (piano), Columbia M2S-693.
3. Kipnis (harpsichord), Angel S-36097.

Suites for Solo Cello:
1. Fournier (cello), Archive 198186/8.
2. Starker (cello), Mercury 77002.

Sonatas and Partitas for Solo Violin:
1. Menuhin (violin), Angel S-3817.
2. Milstein (violin), Deutsche Grammophon 2709047.

Two-Part Invention 4

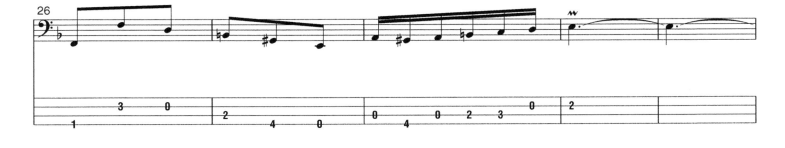

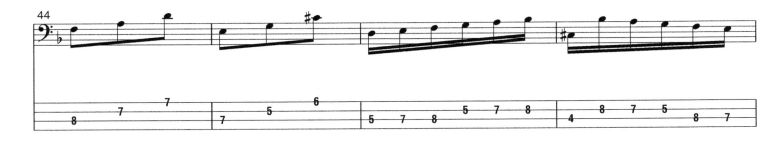

Two-Part Invention 4: Accompaniment

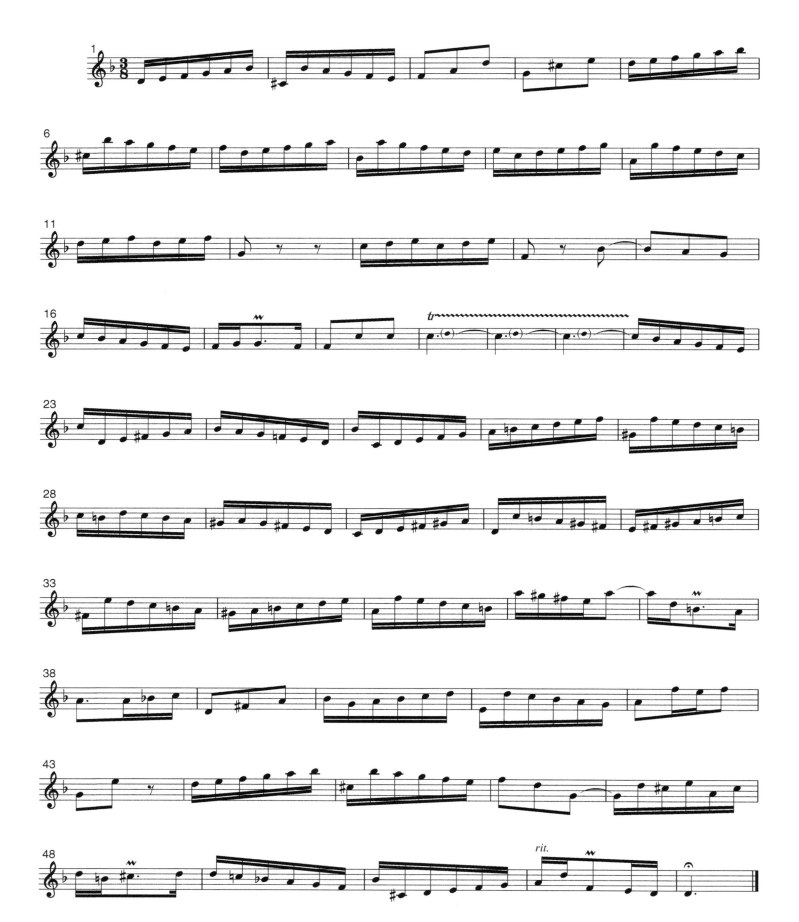

Two - Part Invention 1

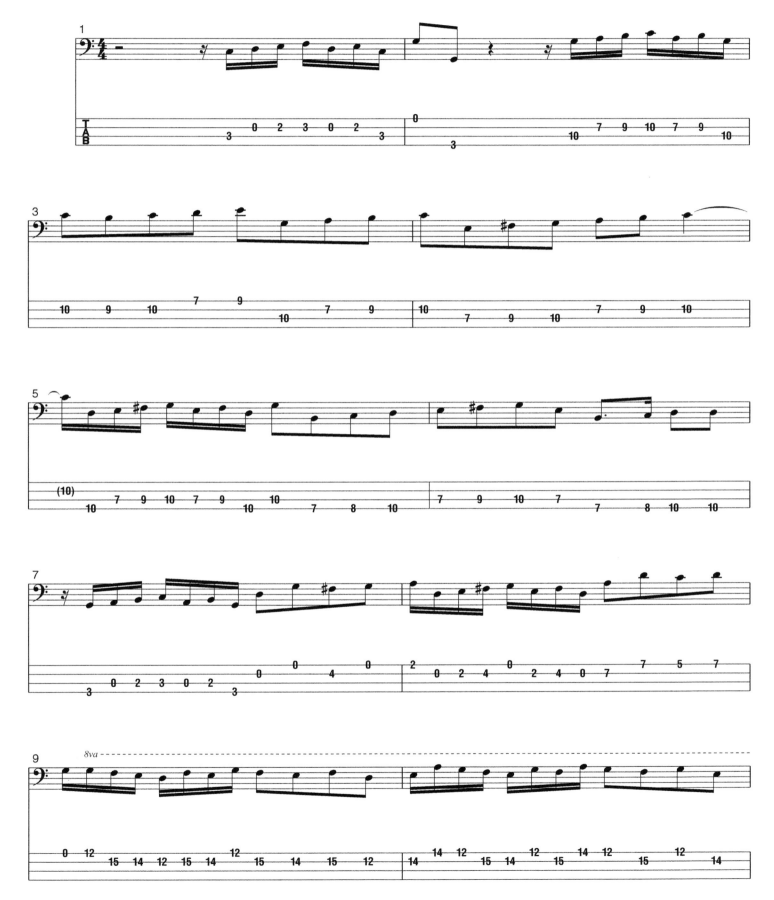

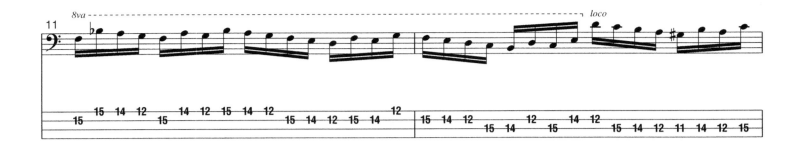

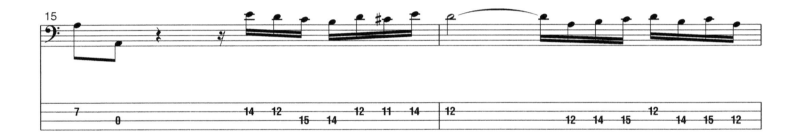

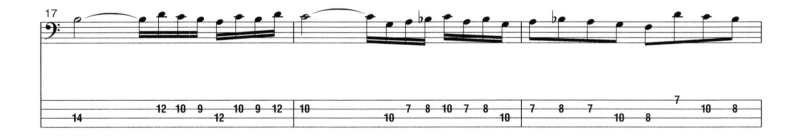

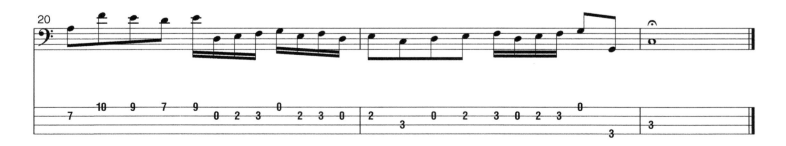

Two-Part Invention 1: Accompaniment

Sinfonia

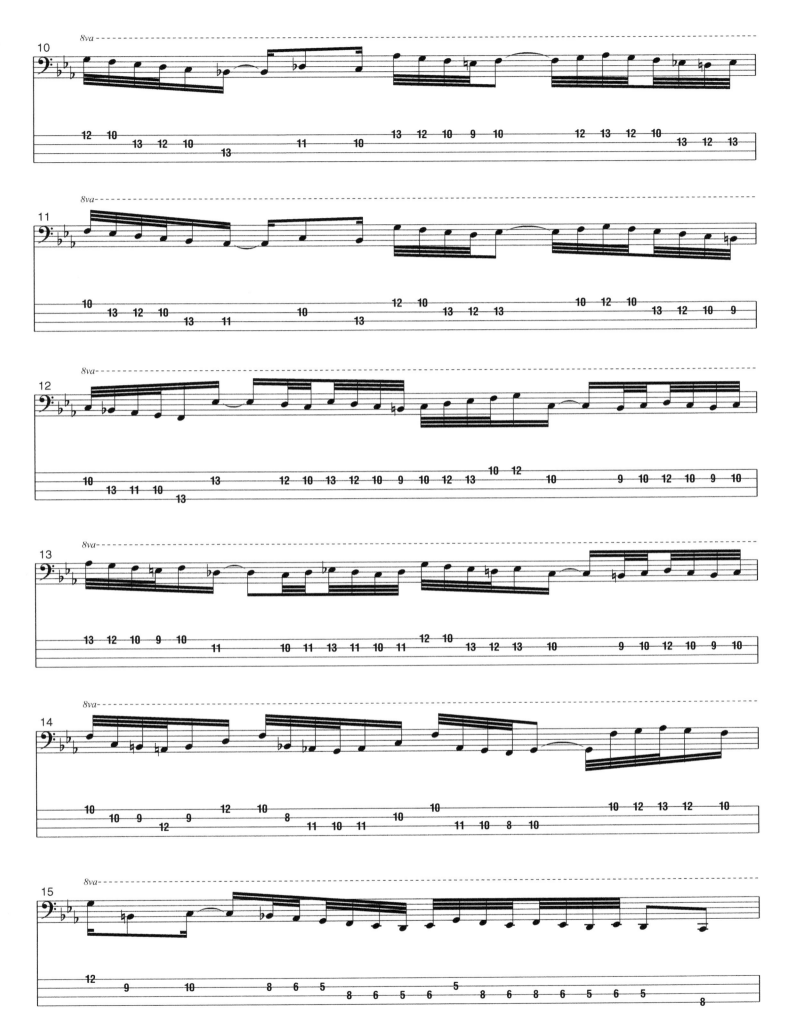

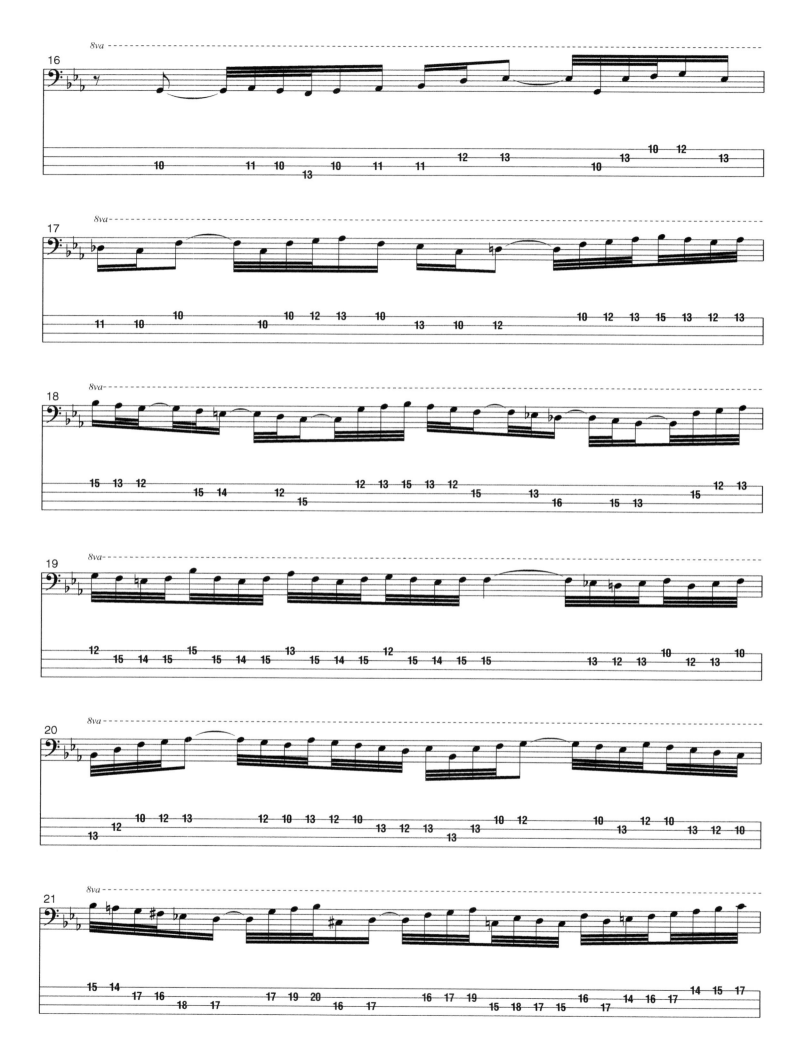

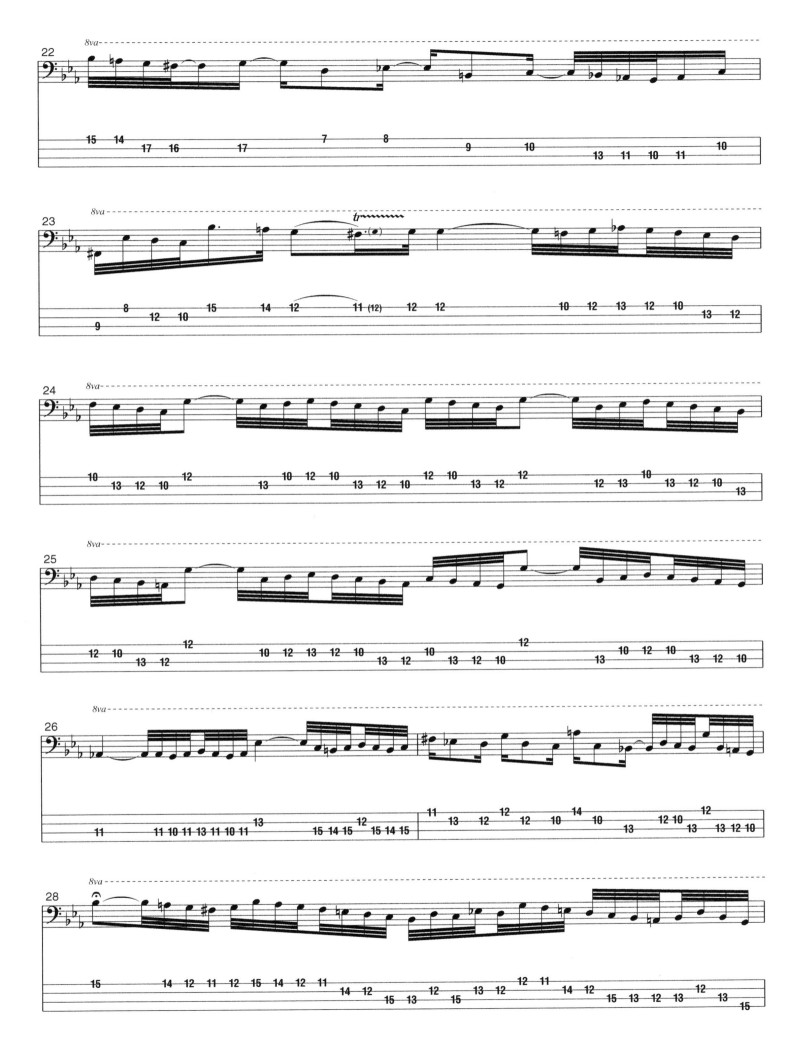

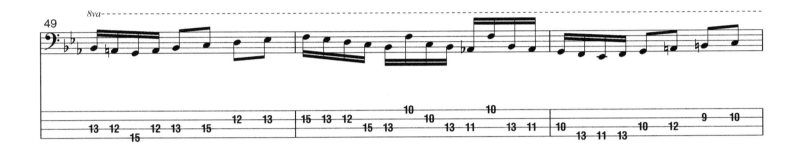

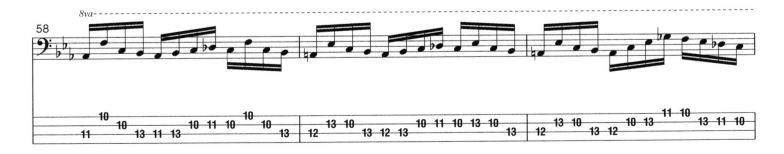

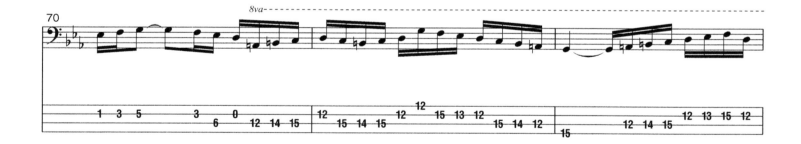

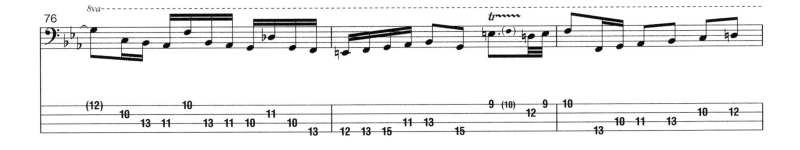

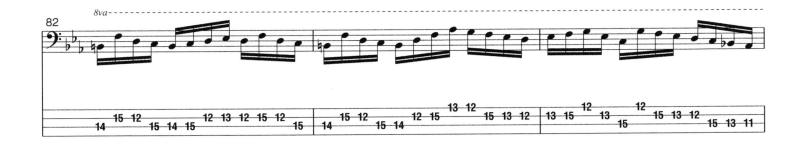

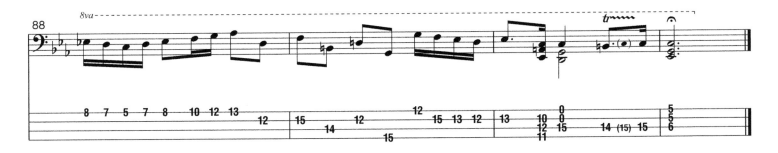

Sinfonia: Accompaniment

Grave Adagio

Andante

19

Bouree 1 & 2

1.

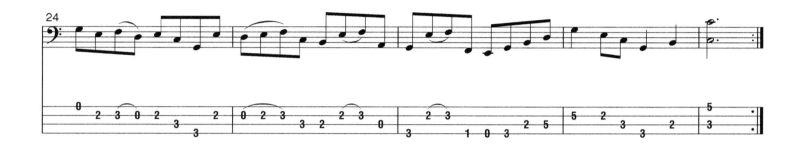

2.

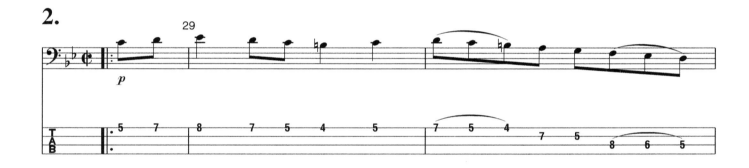

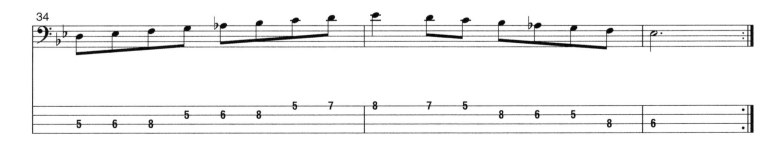

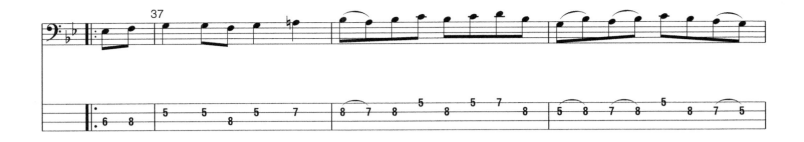

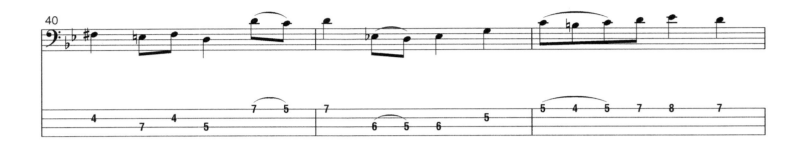

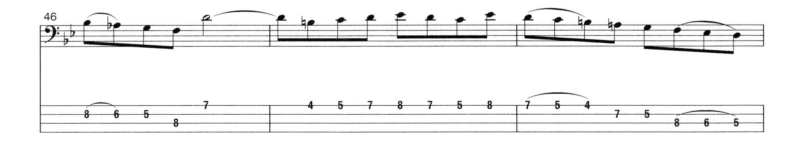

D.C. al Bouree 1

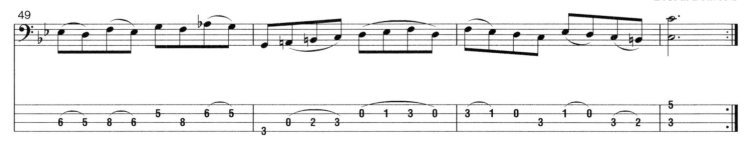

Sarabande

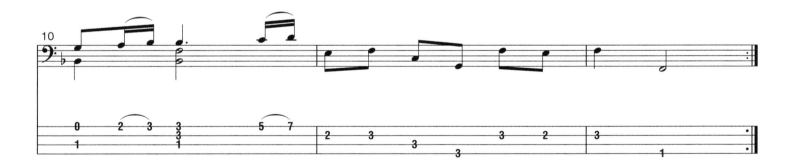

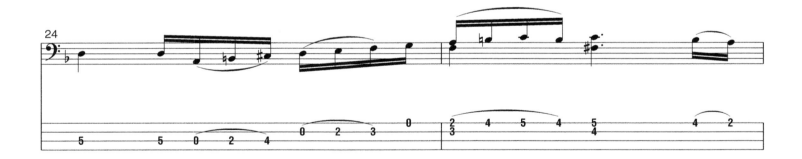

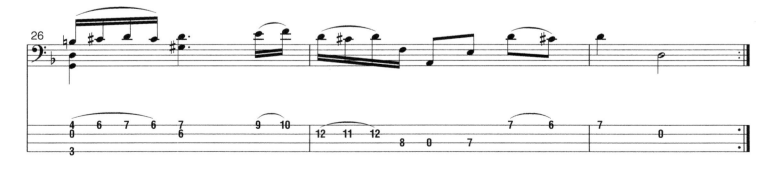

Presto

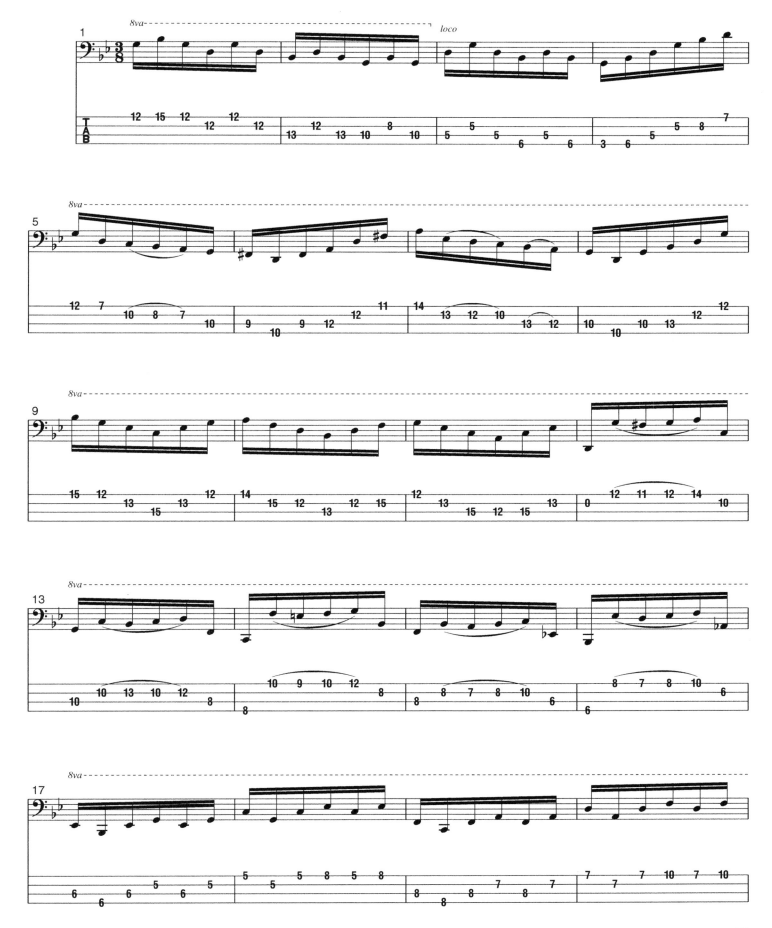

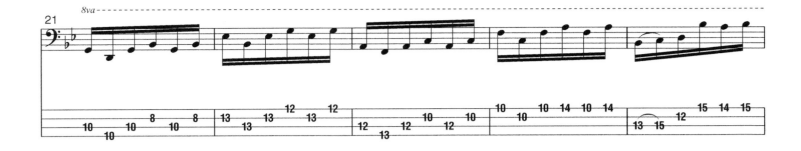

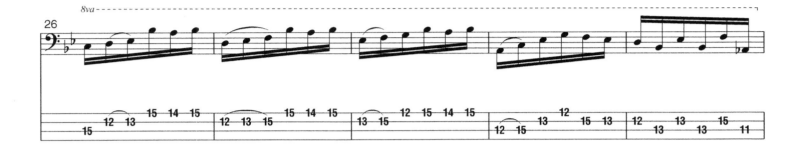

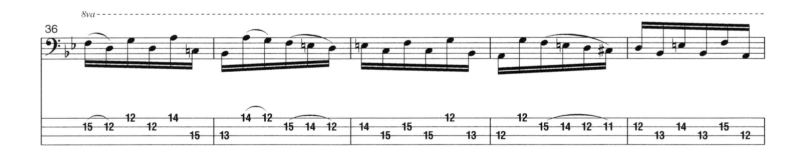

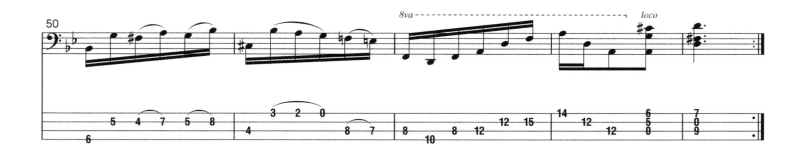

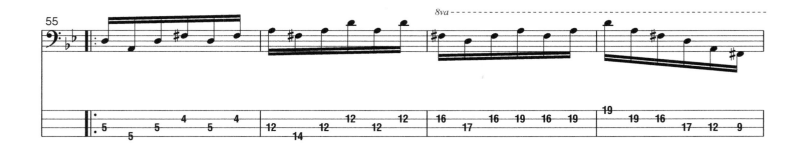

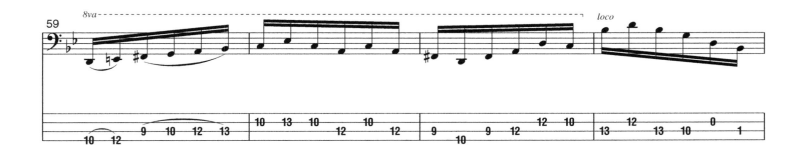

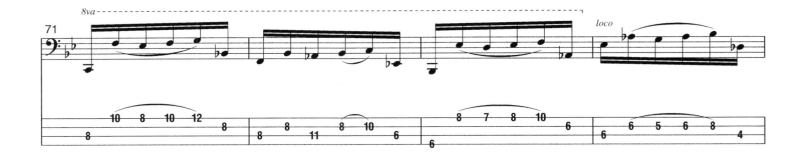

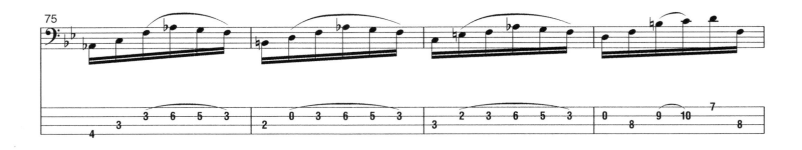

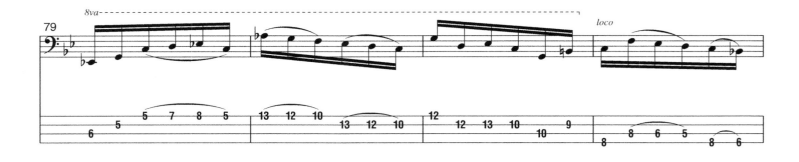

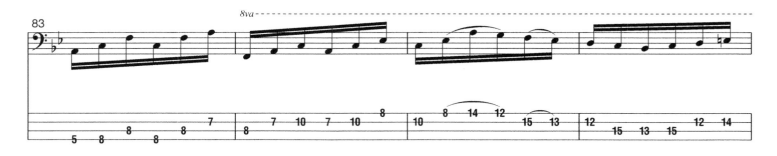

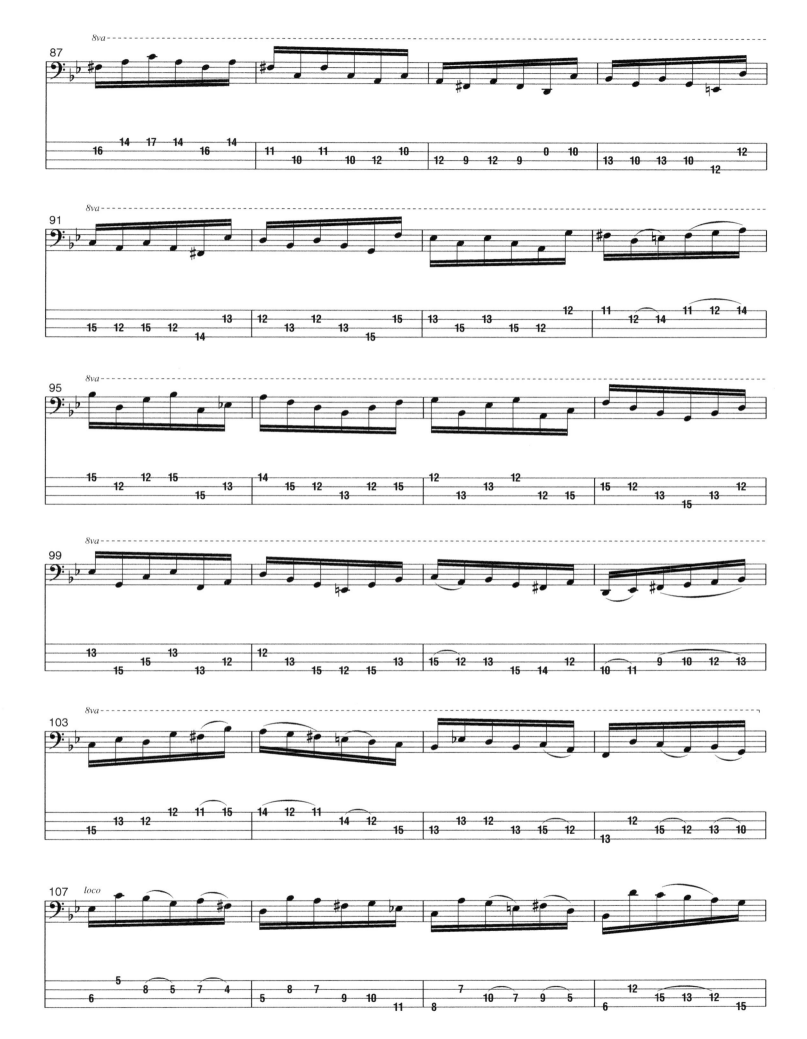

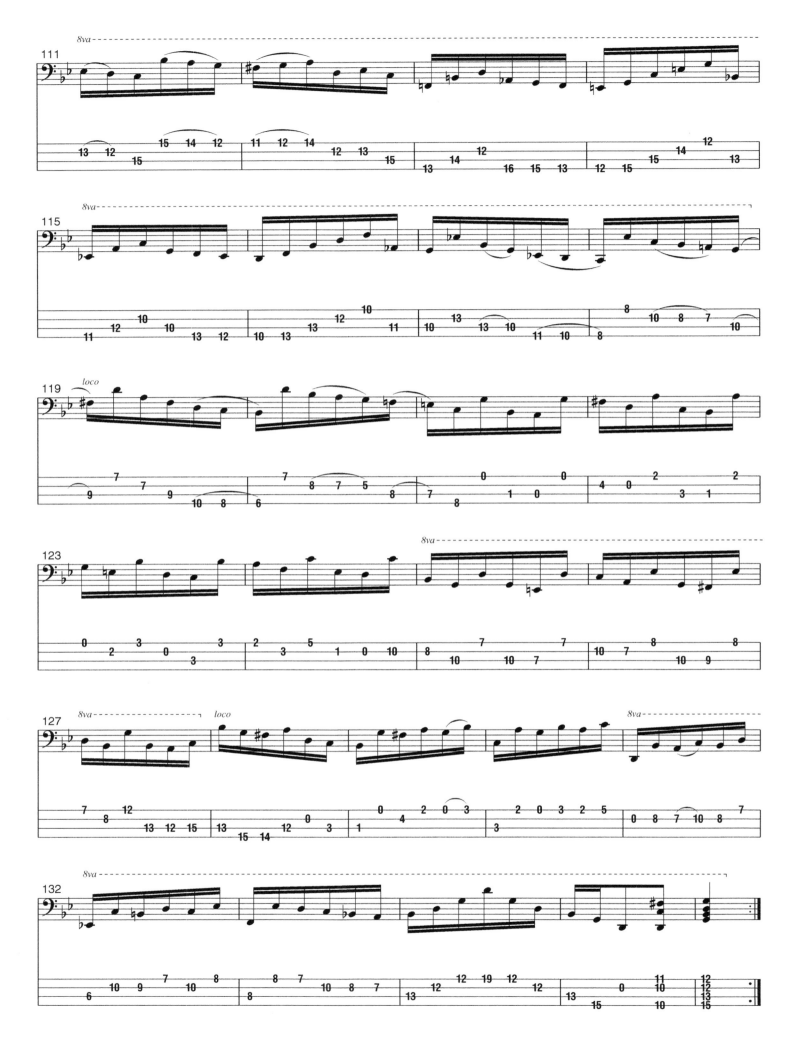

Allemande

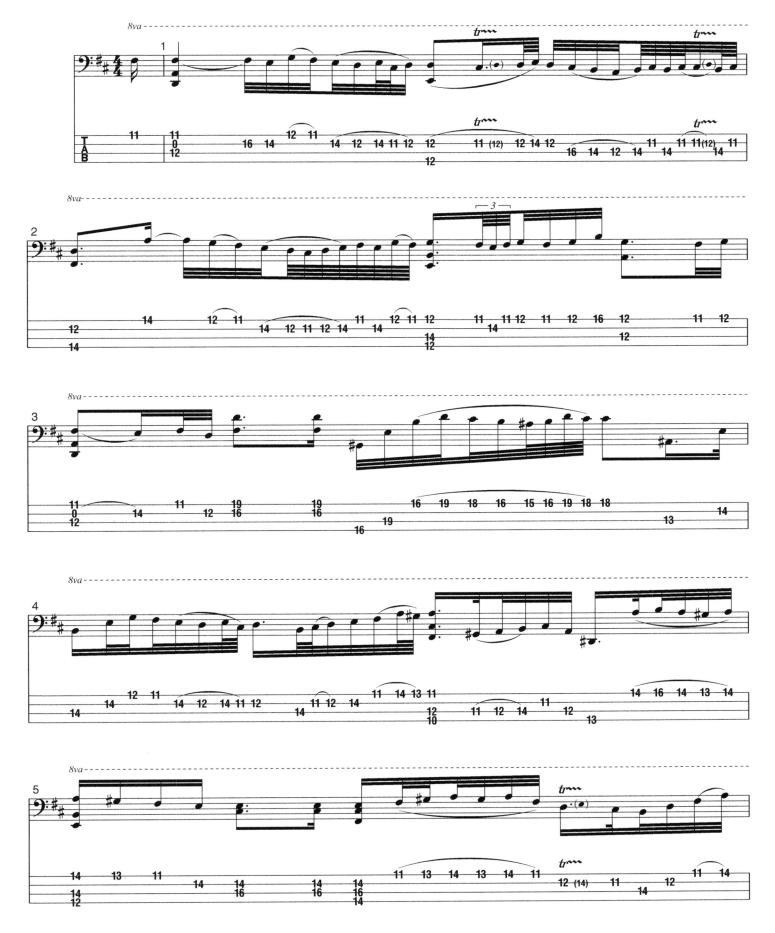

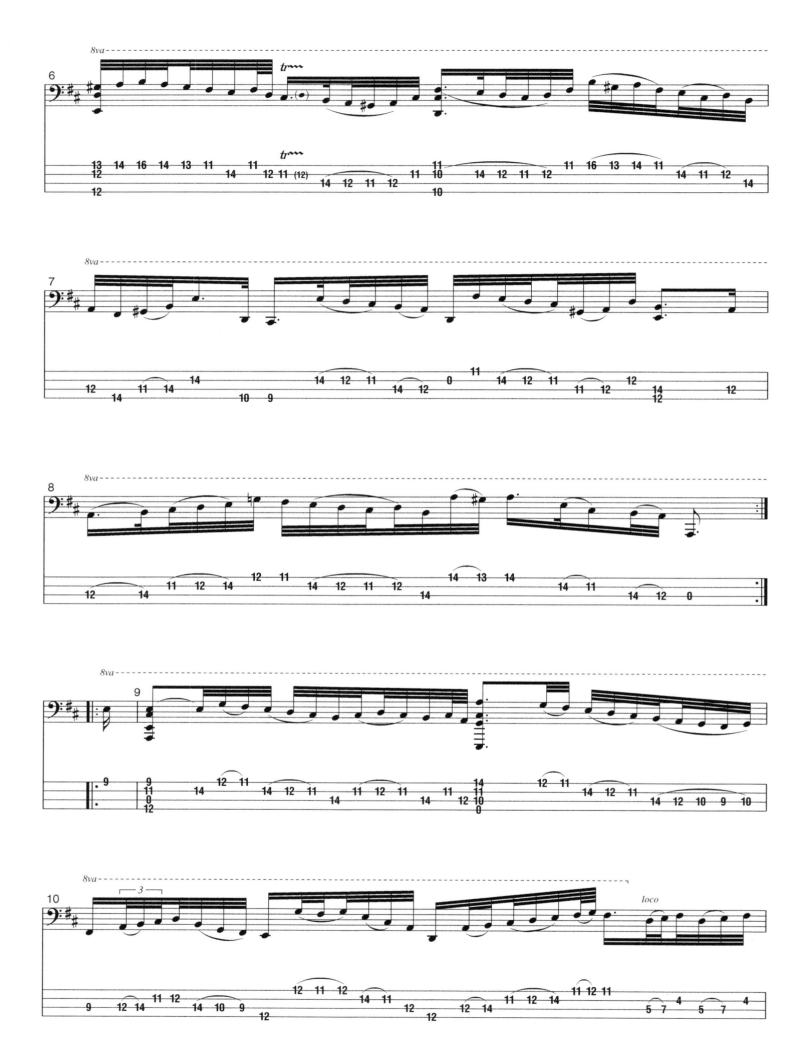

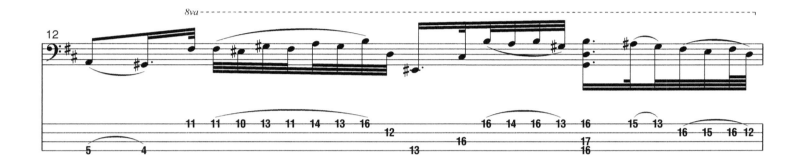

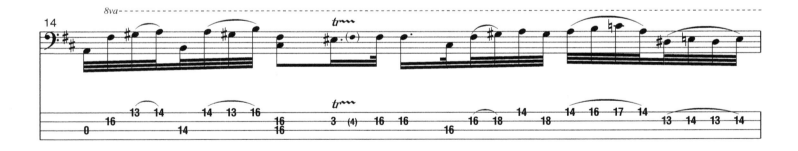

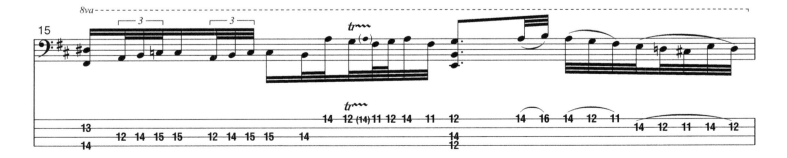

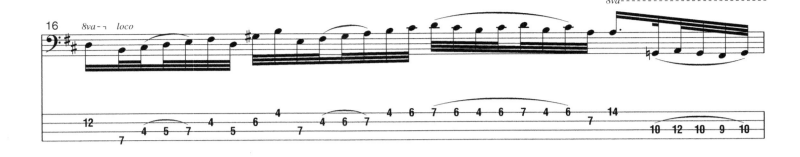

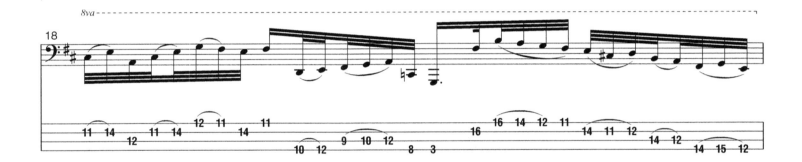

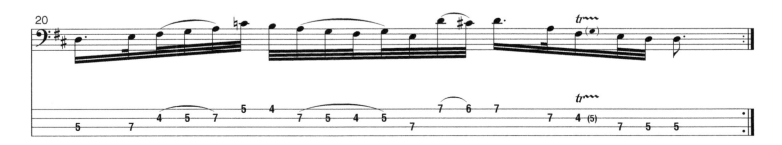

Tempo di Bouree

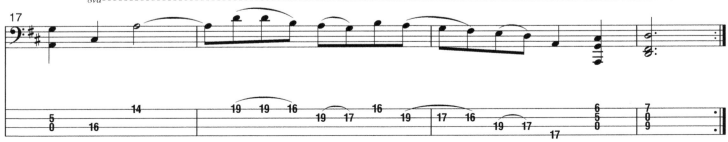

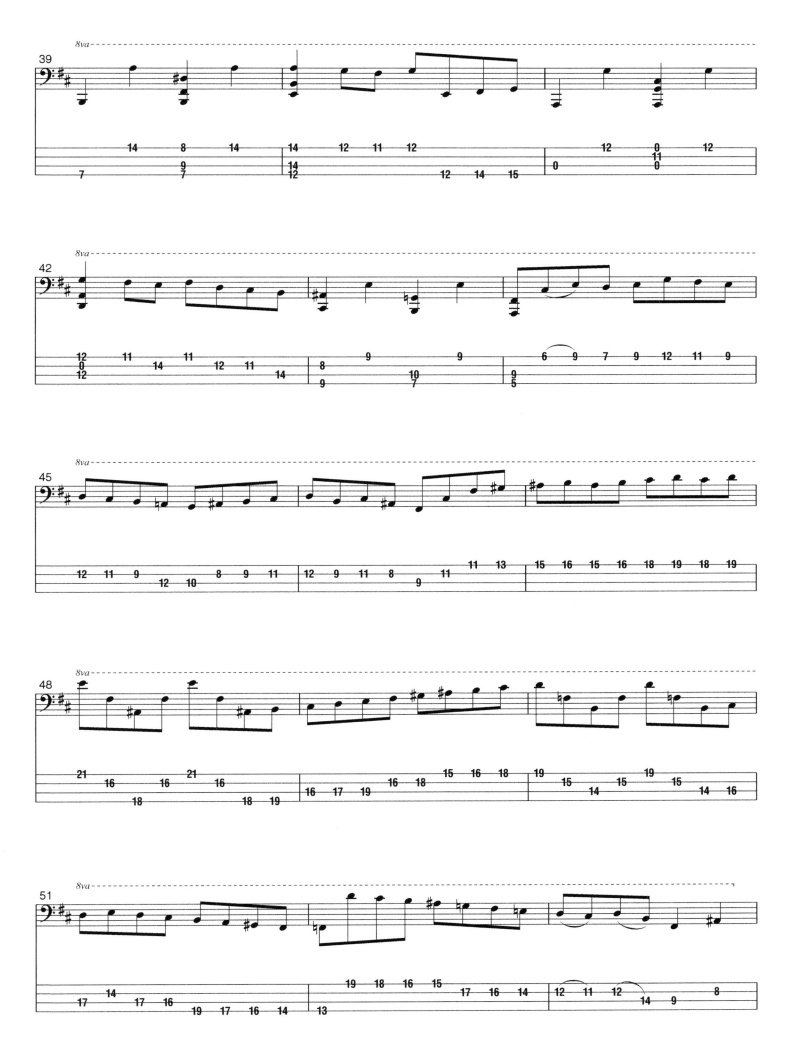

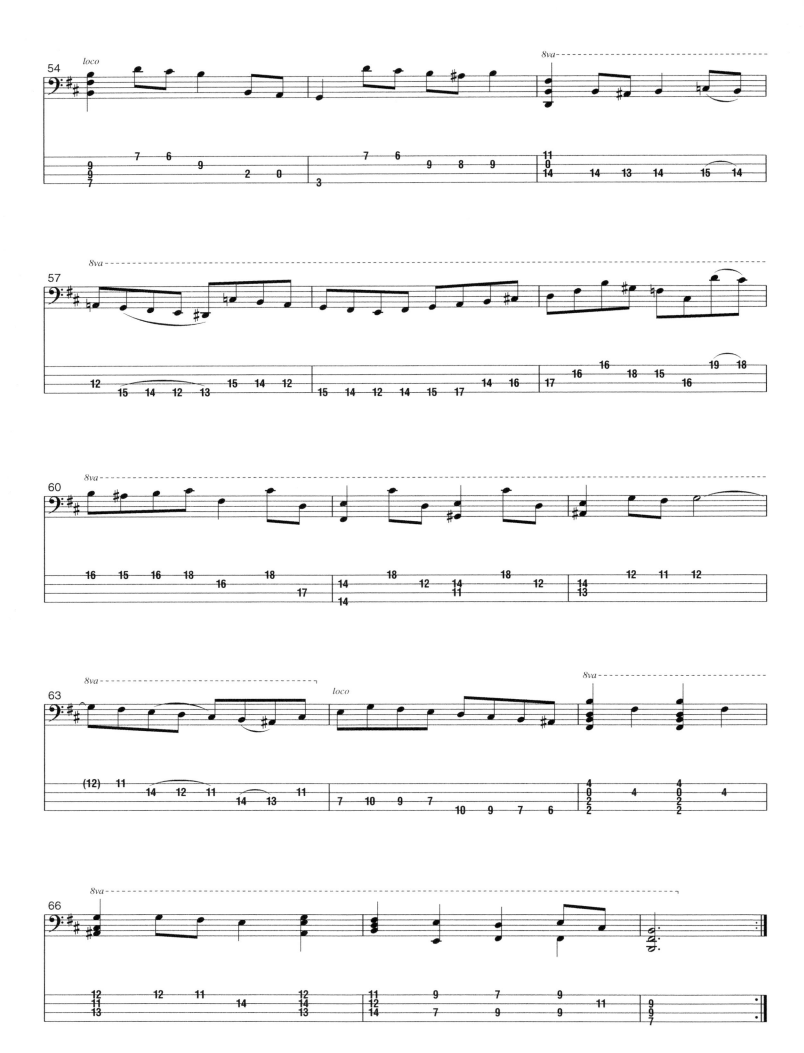